Interim Results from a Study of the Behavior of Juvenile Chinook Salmon at Cougar Reservoir and Dam, Oregon, March–August 2011

By John W. Beeman, Hal C. Hansel, Amy C. Hansen, Philip V. Haner, Jamie M. Sprando, Collin D. Smith, and Scott D. Evans

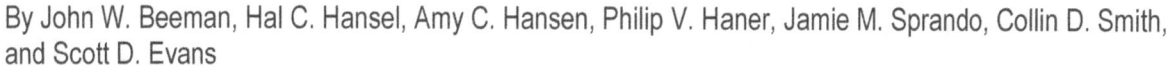

Prepared in cooperation with the U.S. Army Corps of Engineers

Open-File Report 2012–1106

U.S. Department of the Interior
U.S. Geological Survey

U.S. Department of the Interior
KEN SALAZAR, Secretary

U.S. Geological Survey
Marcia K. McNutt, Director

U.S. Geological Survey, Reston, Virginia: 2012

For more information on the USGS—the Federal source for science about the Earth, its natural and living resources, natural hazards, and the environment—visit http://www.usgs.gov or call 1–888–ASK–USGS

For an overview of USGS information products, including maps, imagery, and publications, visit http://www.usgs.gov/pubprod

To order this and other USGS information products, visit http://store.usgs.gov

Suggested citation:
Beeman, J.W., Hansel, H.C., Hansen, A.C., Haner, P.V., Sprando, J.M., Smith, C.D., and Evans, S.D., 2012, Interim results from a study of the behavior of juvenile Chinook salmon at Cougar Reservoir and Dam, Oregon, March–August 2011: U.S. Geological Survey Open-File Report 2012-1106, 30 p.

Contents

Abstract 1
Introduction 1
Methods 3
   Fish Capture, Handling, Tagging, and Release 3
   Vertical Water Reservoir Temperature Profile 4
   Acoustic Telemetry Detection Systems 5
   Data Management and Analysis 7
      Removing False-Positive Records 7
      Dam Passage and Movements within the Reservoir 8
      Probability of Presence near the Temperature Control Tower 10
      Movement Probabilities within the Reservoir 11
Results 11
   Fish Capture, Handling, Tagging, and Release 11
   Environmental Conditions and Dam Operations 12
   Dam Passage and Movements within the Reservoir 14
      Travel Time from Release to the Temperature Control Tower and Release to Dam Passage 15
      Probability of Presence near the Temperature Control Tower 16
      Fish Depths near the Temperature Control Tower 17
      Movement Probabilities within the Reservoir 19
      Fish Behavior during the Reservoir Filling Period 23
      Fish Behavior After the Reservoir Was Full 23
      Fish Behavior During the Spring Test Discharge Period 23
      Effects of Dam Discharge and Diurnal Period on Dam Passage 24
      Discussion 25
Acknowledgments 27
References Cited 27
Appendix A. Fish health reports of yearling Chinook salmon submitted during spring and summer 2011 from Cougar Reservoir, Oregon 29

Figures

Figure 1. Locations of zones bounded by arrays of autonomous acoustic receivers (yellow circles) deployed in Cougar Reservoir, Oregon, 2011 4
Figure 2. Photograph showing locations of cabled hydrophones nearest the temperature control tower at Cougar Dam, Oregon, 2011 6
Figure 3. Locations of hydrophones deployed from floating platforms near the temperature control tower at Cougar Dam, Oregon, 2011. 7
Figure 4. Diagram of zones used in analyses of data based on three-dimensional position estimates of fish at Cougar Dam, Oregon 8
Figure 5. Graphs of total dam discharge and head above the weir gates (top) and forebay elevation and water temperature (bottom) at Cougar Dam, Oregon, 2011 13
Figure 6. Vertical temperature profiles of Cougar Reservoir, Oregon, collected at the boat restricted zone and the fish release site from April 6 to August 4, 2011 14

Figure 7. Hour of last detection of juvenile Chinook salmon with acoustic transmitters released during the spring at Cougar Dam, Oregon assigned dam passage, by rearing type and reservoir filling or full periods, 2011 15

Figure 8. Time (days) from release to first detection at the temperature control tower (left) and time (days) from release to passage (right) for hatchery (solid line) and wild (dotted line) juvenile Chinook salmon release during the spring at Cougar Dam, Oregon, 2011 15

Figure 9. Cumulative probabilities (± 95-percent confidence interval) of being present at least once at reservoir arrays 1, 2, 3, and 5, and at arrays 6 and 7 near the temperature control tower, Cougar Dam, Oregon, 2011 17

Figure 10. Three-dimensional fish position estimates from tagged fish near the temperature control tower at Cougar Dam, Oregon, 2011 18

Figure 11. Least-squares mean depths (± 1 SE) of hatchery (solid line) and wild (dotted line) yearling Chinook salmon tagged with acoustic transmitters during the spring, Cougar Dam, Oregon, 2011. 19

Figure 12. Transition probabilities of hatchery fish released during the spring, Cougar Dam, Oregon, 2011.............. 20

Figure 13. Transition probabilities of wild fish released in the spring, Cougar Dam, Oregon, 2011 21

Figure 14. Graph of movements of several randomly selected fish released in the spring showing directionality in Cougar Reservoir, Oregon, 2011 22

Tables

Table 1. Summary statistics of fork length (mm) and weight (g) of hatchery and wild juvenile Chinook salmon acoustic- and PIT-tagged during spring, Cougar Reservoir, Oregon, 2011 11

Table 2. Summary statistics of fork length (mm) and weight (g) by the different collection methods used to capture wild Chinook salmon during the spring, Cougar Reservoir, Oregon, 2011... 12

Table 3. Suite of models of detection probabilities for the analysis of presence probabilities, Cougar Dam, Oregon, 2011.. 16

Table 4. Suite of models used in estimation of presence probabilities, Cougar Dam, Oregon, 2011 17

Table 5. Regression coefficients from analysis of the effects of discharge and diel period on the rate of dam passage of fish within 74 meters of the face of the temperature control tower, Cougar Dam, Oregon, 2011 25

Conversion Factors and Datums

Conversion Factors

Inch/Pound to SI

Multiply	By	To obtain
foot (ft)	0.3048	meter (m)
cubic foot per second (ft^3/s)	0.02832	cubic meter per second (m^3/s)

SI to Inch/Pound

Multiply	By	To obtain
centimeter (cm)	0.3937	inch (in.)
millimeter (mm)	0.03937	inch (in.)
kilometer (km)	0.6214	mile (mi)
meter (m)	3.281	foot (ft)
cubic meter (m^3)	35.31	cubic foot (ft^3)
kilometer (km)	0.5400	mile, nautical (nmi)
meter per second (m/s)	3.281	foot per second (ft/s)
milliliter (mL)	0.0002642	gallon (gal)
liter (L)	0.2642	gallon (gal)
gram (g)	0.03527	ounce, avoirdupois (oz)

Temperature in degrees Celsius (°C) may be converted to degrees Fahrenheit (°F) as follows:
°F=(1.8×°C)+32.

Datums

Vertical coordinate information is referenced to the National Geodetic Vertical Datum of 1929 (NGVD 29).

Horizontal coordinate information is referenced to the World Geodetic System of 1984 (WGS 84).

Elevation, as used in this report, refers to distance above the vertical datum.

Interim Results from a Study of the Behavior of Juvenile Chinook Salmon at Cougar Reservoir and Dam, Oregon, March–August 2011

By John W. Beeman, Hal C. Hansel, Amy C. Hansen, Philip V. Haner, Jamie M. Sprando, Collin D. Smith, and Scott D. Evans

Abstract

The movements and dam passage of yearling juvenile Chinook salmon implanted with acoustic transmitters and passive integrated transponder tags were studied at Cougar Reservoir and Dam, near Springfield, Oregon. A total of 411 hatchery fish and 26 wild fish were tagged and released between March 7 and May 21, 2011. A series of 16 autonomous hydrophones placed throughout the reservoir were used to determine general fish movements over the life of the acoustic transmitter, which was expected to be 91 days. Movements within the reservoir were directional, and it was common for fish to migrate repeatedly from the head of the reservoir downstream to the dam outlet and back. The dam passage rate was 11.2 percent (95-percent confidence interval 7.8–14.6 percent) for hatchery fish and 15.4 percent (95-percent confidence interval -1.0–31.8 percent) for wild fish within 91 days from release. Most fish passage occurred at night. The median time from release to dam passage was 34.5 days for hatchery fish and 34.2 days for wild fish. A system of hydrophones near the dam outlet, a temperature control tower, was used to estimate positions of fish in three dimensions to enable detailed analyses of fish behavior near the tower. Analyses of these data indicate that hourly averaged depths of fish within a distance of 74 m from the upstream face of the tower ranged from 0.6 to 9.6 meters, with a median depth of 3.6 meters for hatchery fish and 3.4 meters for wild fish. Dam discharge rates and the diurnal period affected the rates of dam passage. Rates of dam passage were similar when the dam discharge rate was less than 1,200 cubic feet per second, but increased sharply at higher discharges. The rate of dam passage at night was 4.4–7.8 times greater than during the day, depending on the distance of fish from the dam. This report is an interim summary of data collected as of August 3, 2011, for planning purposes.

Introduction

The U.S. Army Corps of Engineers (COE) operates the Willamette Project (Project) located in western Oregon, including a series of dams, revetments, and hatcheries. The primary purpose of the Project is flood control, but it also is operated to provide hydroelectricity, irrigation water, navigation, instream flows for wildlife, and recreation. The Project includes 13 dams, about 68 km of revetments, and several fish hatcheries. Cougar Dam and several others are located on tributaries of the Willamette River. The National Oceanic and Atmospheric Administration (2008) determined that the project jeopardizes the sustainability of anadromous fish stocks in the Willamette River Basin.

Cougar Dam is a 158-m-high rock-fill dam on the South Fork of the McKenzie River, located about 63 km east of Springfield, Oregon. The dam, completed in 1964, is owned and operated by the COE. It has a hydraulic capacity of 1,050 ft³/s and two Francis turbine units capable of generating a total of 25 megawatts. The dam also has a spillway with Tainter gates and a temperature control tower installed in 2005 that passes water to a flow regulating outlet (RO) and the powerhouse penstock. The reservoir is used primarily for flood control; therefore, the forebay elevation is maintained at high levels during summer months and low levels during winter months. A maximum conservation pool elevation of 1,690 ft National Geodetic Vertical Datum of 1929 (NGVD 29) typically is reached in May, and a minimum flood-control pool elevation of 1,532 ft NGVD 29 is usually reached in December. All water passing the powerhouse enters the temperature control tower and passes either through the RO intake, at elevation 1,478 ft NGVD 29, or the penstock to the turbines, at elevation 1,420 ft NGVD 29. The temperature control tower allows the use of water from various depths in the forebay to provide water temperatures suitable for salmon in areas downstream of the dam. A fish ladder and trapping facility completed in 2011 collects adult salmon in the tailrace for transportation upstream and provides a means of upstream passage of adult salmon. At the time of this report there was no passage route designed for downstream passage of juvenile salmon.

The 2008 Willamette Biological Opinion requires improvements to operations and structures to reduce impacts on Upper Willamette River (UWR) Chinook salmon (*Oncorhynchus tshawytscha*) and UWR steelhead (*Onchorhynchus mykiss*) (National Oceanic and Atmospheric Administration, 2008). The Opinion includes a requirement to install fish passage facilities (or operational alternatives) at Cougar Dam by 2014, if studies show that installation is feasible. There is little or no information about when and where juvenile Chinook salmon are in various areas of the reservoir and forebay, and, therefore, little information to inform decisions about suitable downstream passage solutions.

The study summarized in this report was designed to quantify juvenile Chinook salmon behavior in the reservoir and near the temperature control tower to help understand their spatial and temporal movements in those areas. Juvenile Chinook salmon, implanted with acoustic transmitters with an expected life of 91 d, were the basis for inference. The study is designed to collect data from fish released in March, April, and May 2011, and again in September, October, and November 2011. This report is a summary of the data collected from fish tagged during March, April, and May 2011 for use by fishery managers and others requiring interim results for planning purposes.

The study was designed to address four objectives:

1. To determine the spatial and temporal distribution of juvenile Chinook salmon in the Cougar Dam forebay near the temperature control tower;

2. To determine the spatial and temporal movements of juvenile Chinook salmon throughout the reservoir;

3. To determine if juvenile Chinook salmon of hatchery origin can be used as surrogates for naturally produced juvenile Chinook salmon;

Methods

Fish Capture, Handling, Tagging, and Release

The data described in this report were collected from yearling juvenile Chinook salmon tagged with acoustic transmitters and passive integrated transponder (PIT) tags. The tagged fish included those of hatchery and wild origins. Hatchery-origin fish were obtained from the McKenzie River Hatchery in Leaburg, Oregon, and wild origin fish were collected from within Cougar Reservoir.

Approximately 650 hatchery fish were sorted by size at McKenzie River Hatchery and placed into one-half of a full-length raceway in February 2011 to meet a minimum fork length requirement of 95 mm per regional agreement (Surgical Protocols Steering Committee, 2011). The raceway was supplied with flowing river water. On 1 or 2 d every other week in March, April, and May, fish were netted from the raceway and placed into a 264-L transport tank and taken to the tagging site at the Cougar Dam adult fish facility, where they were held between 17.3 and 25.5 h prior to tagging. The recommendations of the Surgical Protocols Steering Committee (2011) were followed in all aspects of the fish holding, tagging, and releasing procedures.

Wild fish were captured using a Lampara seine and an Oneida Lake trap. The Lampara seine was 91.4 m long and fished to a depth of approximately 7.6 m. The Lampara seine was fished by deploying the net from a boat, encircling an area, and then hauling the net back onto the boat deck. The Oneida Lake trap net, operated by the Oregon Department of Fish and Wildlife, is a passive capture method, and was constructed from 0.64-cm mesh and consisted of a 2.4-m^3 holding box, with a 3.4-m × 3.0-m lead net, and two 7.2-m × 3.0-m wings. The net generally is set near the shore, and anchored to stabilize it from wind and wave action. All fish collected were held in an aerated container supplied with fresh reservoir water, and then transported to the Cougar Dam adult fish facility and treated in the same manner as the hatchery fish.

Transmitter implantation and fish recovery were completed near the Cougar Dam adult fish facility. Fish were considered suitable for tagging if they were free of major injuries, had no external signs of gas-bubble trauma or fungus, were less than or equal to 20 percent descaled, and were not previously tagged with acoustic or PIT tags. To implant the transmitter, fish were anesthetized using buffered tricane methanesulfonate (Argent Chemical Laboratories, Redmond, Washington) at a concentration of 75–80 mg/L. Fish weight and length were measured immediately prior to the surgery. The acoustic transmitters were 12 mm high × 5.21 mm wide × 3.77 mm deep, had a mass of 0.43 g in air and 0.29 g in water, and a had a volume of 0.14 mL. Expected transmitter life at the nominal pulse-rate interval of 17 s was 91 d. A 23-mm-long PIT tag weighing 0.10 g was placed inside the body cavity along with the acoustic transmitter. All weighing, measuring, and containment equipment were treated with a 0.25 mL/L concentration of Stress Coat® (Aquarium Pharmaceuticals, Inc., Chalfont, Pennsylvania) to reduce handling-related stress to the fish through electrolyte loss. Fish were placed in a 19 L perforated recovery bucket filled with 7 L of river water immediately after surgery. Dissolved oxygen concentrations were maintained between 80 and 100 percent of saturation during recovery. Each recovery bucket held up to three fish. Fish were watched periodically during the first 10 min after surgery to ensure they recovered from anesthesia. Recovery buckets were then fitted with lids and placed in a raceway provided with flowing river water, where fish were held for 19.1–25.2 h prior to release. The recovery buckets were floated in the raceway using rubber inner tubes around the top to allow fish access to air to adjust their buoyancy.

Tagged fish were released near the head of Cougar Reservoir. After the recovery period, fish were taken by boat upstream through Cougar Reservoir to the release site about halfway between the two shorelines near the Slide Creek boat ramp (fig. 1). Recovery buckets were removed from the raceway, inspected for mortalities, and transferred to an insulated, 1,556-L plastic tank. Two tanks were mounted on a flatbed trailer with lids to limit water spillage during transport. Each tank was filled with river water and the fish were driven about 11.4 km to the boat ramp. Recovery buckets were then transferred to a boat and taken upstream approximately 7.0 river kilometers to the release site. Water-quality measurements were recorded to assess the water temperature difference between the recovery bucket and the reservoir; tempering was performed when the difference was greater than $2°C$ (Surgical Protocols Steering Committee, 2011). Fish were released by partially submerging the buckets in the reservoir and gently tipping them over so the fish could swim out.

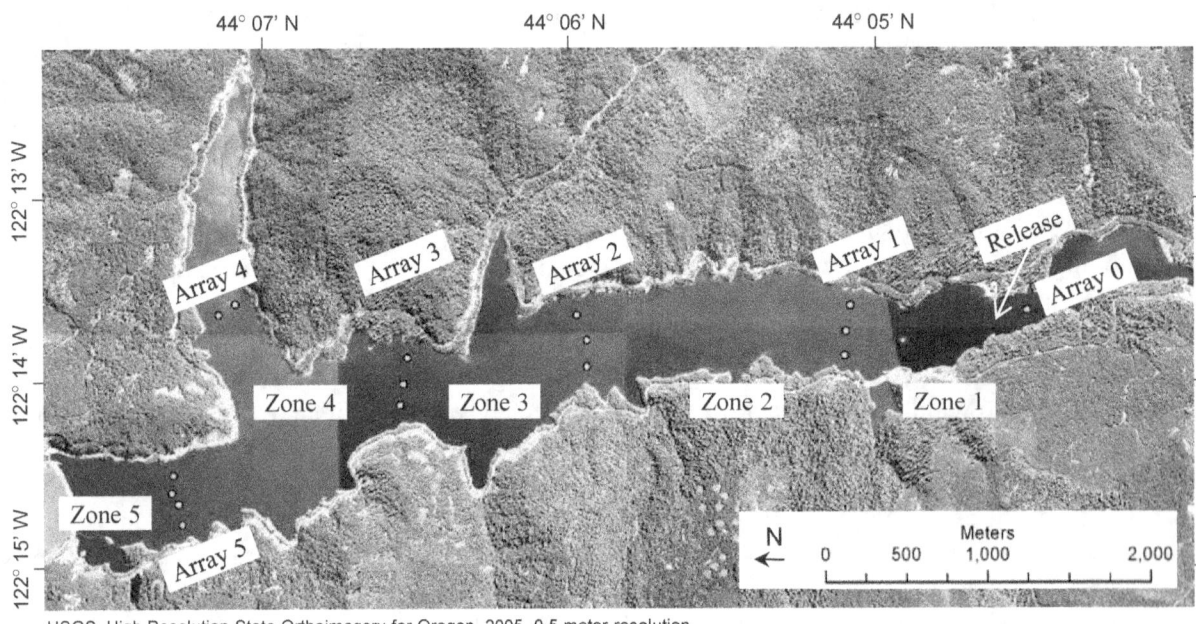

USGS High Resolution State Orthoimagery for Oregon, 2005, 0.5 meter resolution

Figure 1. Locations of zones bounded by arrays of autonomous acoustic receivers (yellow circles) deployed in Cougar Reservoir, Oregon, 2011. A white arrow indicates the release location.

Vertical Water Reservoir Temperature Profile

Water temperature profiles were measured periodically near the log boom at the boat restricted-zone line and near the fish-release site. Measurements were recorded on seven dates from April 6 to August 4, 2011, near the boat restricted-zone line, and on five dates from May 5 to August 4, 2011, near the release site. Measurements were recorded by slowly lowering (about 0.5 m/s) a continuously recording bathythermograph (Model OS 200, Ocean Sensors, Inc.©, San Diego, California) from the reservoir surface to the bottom. Reservoir depths were recorded in feet, following local convention. Water temperatures also are recorded hourly by the COE at approximately 2-m intervals using an automated series of thermistors located at the southeastern corner of the temperature control tower.

Acoustic Telemetry Detection Systems

Signals from acoustic transmitters were detected using two types of Juvenile Salmon Acoustic Telemetry System hydrophone systems provided by the COE. Acoustic signals from tagged fish in the reservoir, from about the log boom at the boat-restricted zone upstream to the head of the reservoir, were detected using autonomous hydrophones spaced across the reservoir's width at six locations (fig. 1). These hydrophones operate independently and record the presence of a transmitter when it is within range. We empirically determined that in the eastern arm of the reservoir, 82 percent of the expected number of transmissions were detected at a range of 105 m, and 10 percent were detected at a range of 180 m. Based on these data, the hydrophones were spaced about 100 m from shorelines and 200 m from each other at a depth of no more than about 33 mm from the water surface along lines across the reservoir (hereafter called "arrays"). Hydrophone depths were readjusted during biweekly visits to change batteries and download data. Several hydrophones were moored at depths greater than 33 m from the water surface during March 2011. Hydrophones were deployed with steel anchors and float lines until April 2011, when deployment was changed to acoustic release mechanisms using methods similar to those described by Titzler and others (2010), except that we used burlap bags of sand as anchors. The entire suite of 16 autonomous hydrophones was operational beginning on March 10, 2011.

Acoustic signals from tagged fish near the temperature control tower were detected using three 4-hydrophone systems linked to one another using a common clock. Each of these systems included four hydrophones connected with cables to a common computer. Each computer received its system time from a global positioning system. A similar cabled hydrophone system is described by Weiland and others (2009). The use of a common time for all hydrophones allows estimation of fish position based on time of signal arrival if hydrophone locations and the speed of sound in the study area are known. The study was designed to use a laser-based system of estimating hydrophone positions, but purchasing delays required the use of a global positioning system-based method, which was installed on April 21, 2011, at 4 p.m.

The cabled hydrophone systems were installed on the temperature control tower at several elevations and from floating platforms (figs. 2 and 3). The hydrophones at the lowest two elevations were installed beginning in January and became operational on March 17, 2011, after cables to connect the hydrophones to the computers were delivered per COE contract. The remaining cabled hydrophones became operational as the water elevation increased to the planned installation elevation (for hydrophones affixed to the tower), or as equipment became available (for hydrophones deployed from floating platforms). The eight hydrophones nearest the tower were all operational by April 5, 2011, and the entire system of cabled hydrophones was operational on April 21, 2011. Data prior to the installation of the hydrophone positioning system (April 21, 2011) is suitable for analyses based on presence or absence of tagged fish, but cannot be used for estimating fish positions. The range of the cabled hydrophone systems was assumed to be similar to that of the autonomous hydrophones. This assumption seems reasonable because each transmitter message typically was detected by nearly all hydrophones, which were spaced about 80 m apart.

Figure 2. Photograph showing locations of cabled hydrophones nearest the temperature control tower at Cougar Dam, Oregon, 2011. Round symbols represent hydrophones affixed to the tower, and square symbols indicate those mounted from floating platforms. Numbers are hydrophone elevations. Dotted lines represent approximate locations of full and minimum conservation pool water elevations of 515 and 468 meters. Photograph taken during construction in 2005 provided by U.S. Army Corps of Engineers, and inset photographs taken by Amy Hansen and Scott Evans of the U.S. Geological Survey.

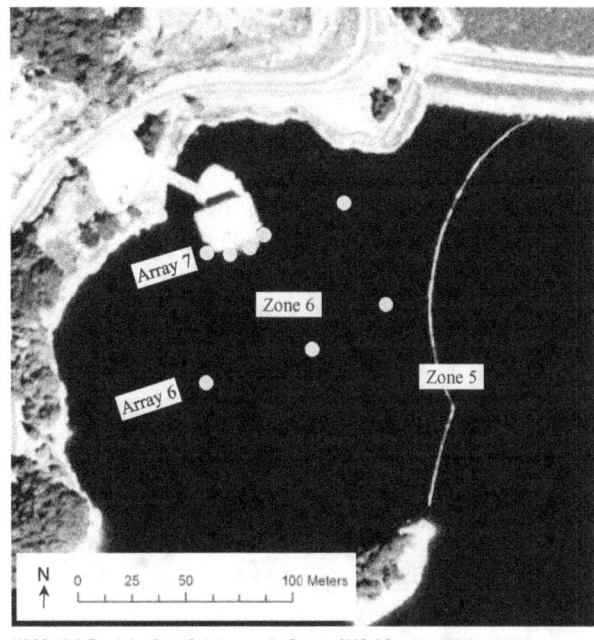

USGS High Resolution State Orthoimagery for Oregon, 2005, 0.5 meter resolution

Figure 3. Locations of hydrophones deployed from floating platforms near the temperature control tower at Cougar Dam, Oregon, 2011. Array 7 hydrophones also are represented in figure 2.

Data Management and Analysis

Removing False-Positive Records

Data from the hydrophones were processed to remove false-positive records prior to analysis. False-positive records are those that indicate detection of a transmitter when the transmitter was not present, and are common in active telemetry systems. Procedures developed by the Pacific Northwest National Laboratory (Mark Weiland, written commun., June 17, 2010) were used to remove false-positive records. The steps include removing records from tag codes not released, records suspected of being from reflections of valid tag signals (multipath), and records that are not close to a multiple of the tag pulse interval. Records from the cabled hydrophone system also were required to be present on more than one hydrophone in order to be retained.

A transmitter-life study was conducted to determine how long data from tagged fish could be collected. The tag-life test was conducted using 50 tags in a holding pond at the adult fish facility at Cougar Dam beginning on May 20, 2011. Inasmuch as the results in this report were estimated prior to the completion of the tag-life study, we used the expected tag life specified by the manufacturer, which was 91 d, as the follow-up time when estimating the proportion of tagged fish that passed the dam.

A series of zones were defined to enable analysis of fish movements. Zones were bounded by arrays in the reservoir, or by concentric rings specific distances from the temperature control tower (figs. 1, 3, and 4). General fish movements between arrays over time were plotted as an example of the raw data used in subsequent analyses. Analyses of fish presence (probability of presence at each array and over all arrays between release and the temperature control tower) and movement probabilities (Markov movement probabilities) were based on detections of fish at the arrays. The zones near the temperature control tower were bounded at 10-m intervals from the zone nearest to the tower, which was within 4 m of the tower. These data were used in regressions described in the section Dam Passage and Movements within the Reservoir.

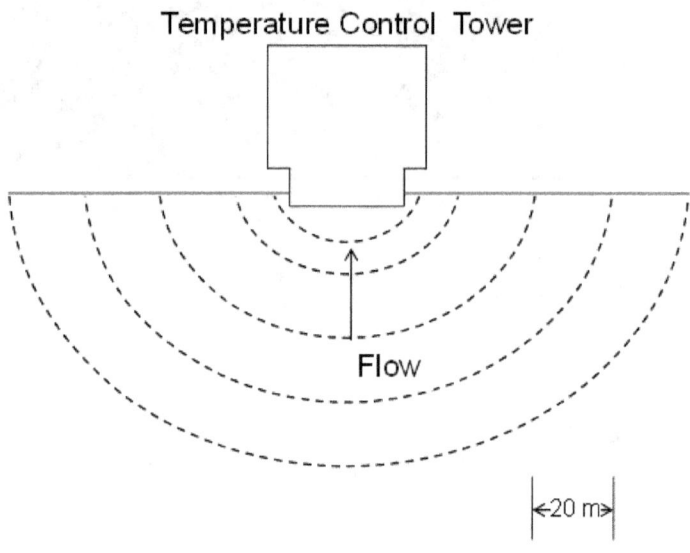

Figure 4. Diagram of zones used in analyses of data based on three-dimensional position estimates of fish at Cougar Dam, Oregon. The areas bounded by the dotted lines (from bottom up) are 74, 54, 34, 14, and 4 meters from the upstream face of the temperature control tower.

Dam Passage and Movements within the Reservoir

Descriptions of fish behavior and an analysis of factors affecting dam passage were based on several time periods. Fish behavior was described during the period of reservoir filling and after it was full, based on differences in dam operations during these periods. The analysis of factors affecting dam passage was divided into two periods: (1) the period of three-dimensional fish position data available beginning April 21, 2011, at 4 p.m., and (2) the week-long discharge test period beginning slightly before that time. The analysis of dam passage during the discharge test period in April was based on an 88-hour period prior to the test, the 176-hour test period from April 15, 2011, at 6 a.m. to April 21, 2011, at 2 p.m., and an 88-hour period following the test for a total time period of April 11, 2011, at 2 p.m. to April 26, 2011, at 6 a.m..

Dam passage was determined using presence data from the cabled hydrophones nearest the temperature control tower. The date and time of dam passage were assigned if the first detection of the last transmitter message was at any of the four hydrophones located on the temperature control tower that were closest to the water surface. This method was chosen to limit passage assignments to fish last detected in the area generally between the water surface and the top of the weir gates, and was consistent with histories of tagged fish known to have passed the dam based on PIT-tag detections downstream. Fish last detected within the cabled hydrophone system less than 93 h prior to the analysis cutoff of 12 p.m. on August 3, 2011, were not assigned passage, because that period of time was shorter than the longest time between last detection of other fish at the cabled hydrophone system and detection elsewhere in the reservoir.

Analyses of the timing and rates of dam passage for fish in the zones described in figure 4 were conducted using time-to-event methods (Hosmer and Lemeshow, 1999; Castro-Santos and Haro, 2003). These methods are ideally suited to analysis of data based on the timing of events, such as travel times, and the rates of event occurrences, such as the guidance, attraction, and passage of fish (Castro-Santos and Haro, 2010).

The time elapsed from fish release to two event types was described using Kaplan-Meier survivorship functions. The events are (1) detection by the cabled hydrophones mounted to the temperature control tower and the two hydrophones mounted on barges directly adjacent to the tower, and (2) dam passage. The survivorship function of a variable T is defined as:

$$S(t) = \Pr\{T > t\} \tag{1}$$

where T is a random variable with a probability distribution, denoting an event time for an individual. If the event of interest is passing a dam, the survivorship function gives the probability of not passing the dam after time t. As such, the median time occurs when the survivorship function equals 0.5. In the absence of censoring, the survivorship function represents the proportion of the population that has not experienced an event (for example, passing the dam). Examining the survivorship function can be useful to describe the timing of events as well as the proportion of the population still at risk of the event at different points in time. Fish that had not experienced an event by the longest-known transmitter life were right censored at that time.

Cox proportional-hazards regression was used to determine the potential effects of dam discharge and diurnal period on the rates of dam passage. In Cox proportional-hazards regression the rates of events are expressed as a hazard function defined as:

$$h(t) = \lim_{\Delta t \to 0} \Pr\{t \leq T < t + 1 \mid T \geq t\} / \Delta t \tag{2}$$

representing the instantaneous risk, or rate, of an event occurring at time t. Equation 2 describes a conditional rate: It is the probability of the event occurring in a limited time interval, conditional on the event having not occurred yet, divided by the length of the interval (which makes it a rate, not a probability) (Allison, 1995). Results are expressed in terms of a hazard ratio that describes the change in the rate of interest for each unit increase in an independent variable. For continuous variables, the hazard rate is interpreted by subtracting 1 from the hazard ratio and multiplying the remainder by 100 percent. For dichotomous variables, the hazard ratio is interpreted directly. For example, a hazard ratio of 1.15 from a continuous covariate indicates that the rate of the event increases 15 percent for each unit increase in the covariate, and a hazard rate of 0.75 indicates a decrease of 25 percent per unit increase in the covariate. A hazard ratio of 2.00 for a dichotomous covariate (for example, day = 0, night = 1) indicates that the rate of the event is twice the value at the higher value relative to the lower value (in this example, at night compared to during the day). Hazards are independent of the size of the population. The counting-process-style data input was used to divide the data into diel period (day or night) and to increment other time-varying covariates by hour (Hosmer and Lemeshow, 1999). The time interval was reset each time an individual entered a new zone or passed the dam. Censor variables of 0 (no event), 1 (downstream movement or dam passage), 2 (upstream movement), or 4 (end of expected tag life) were used in a competing risks analysis focusing on dam passage.

Probability of Presence near the Temperature Control Tower

The probability that a fish was present at each array or at the temperature control tower at least once after release was estimated. The purpose of this analysis was to determine if fish near the head of the reservoir would be available for capture by a juvenile fish collection facility if one were present. This analysis does not indicate if fish that were not detected at an array or near the tower were alive or dead, only that they were never detected in the area of interest. The data were based on the presence or absence of fish detected at the arrays throughout the reservoir or at the cabled hydrophone systems near the tower, which together detect fish within about 200 m of the tower.

The probability of being present near the temperature control tower at least once was estimated using Cormack-Jolly–Seber mark–recapture methods (Cormack, 1964; Jolly, 1965; Seber, 1965) using Program MARK (White and Burnham, 1999). This method primarily is used to estimate survival and recapture probabilities in mark-recapture studies, but in this case, we used it to estimate presence and recapture probabilities. Detection of a tagged animal is the joint probability of presence and being detected when present, so these parameters must be estimated separately. We constructed *a priori* models of presence and recapture probabilities based on differences between hatchery and wild fish and among arrays. In this analysis, the "recapture probability" at an array is the probability of being detected at that array at least once. Overdispersion in the data was estimated using the median c-hat procedure in Program MARK. Models describing different hypotheses about processes driving presence or detection probabilities were evaluated using the Akaike Information Criterion with an adjustment for effects of sample size and overdispersion (QAICc). Burnham and Anderson (2002) suggest that when QAICc values differ by less than 2 units, the support for one hypothesis over another is not meaningfully different based on the data and models considered. They also suggest that QAICc differences of 4–7 indicate considerably less support for the model with the greater QAICc, and differences greater than 10 indicate essentially no support for the model with the greater QAICc. The probability of being present at the temperature control tower at least once was estimated as the product of array-specific presence probabilities, with the standard error estimated using the delta method (Seber, 1982).

The probability of presence was estimated from model-averaged coefficients. A total of four models of recapture probabilities and five models of presence probabilities were considered based on various combinations of fish origin (hatchery or wild) and array.

Movement Probabilities within the Reservoir

The probabilities of upstream and downstream movements at each array were estimated to determine if there were net upstream or downstream movements of fish and if the movements in the reservoir depended on past movements. Transition (movement) probabilities can be used to stochastically predict or simulate future fish movements (Johnson and others, 2004). A Markov-chain analysis was used to determine if movements between reservoir arrays followed a one-step process, by which movement from one array to an adjacent array is not dependent on its previous location (a first-order Markov process; Bhat and Miller, 2002). We estimated the probability of a fish moving from one array to the next as either a first-order, or one-step process (not dependent on previous location) or second order, or two-step process (dependent on previous location), and assessed support of the hypotheses by the data using the Akaike Information Criterion (Burnham and Anderson, 2002).

Results

Fish Capture, Handling, Tagging, and Release

A total of 415 hatchery fish and 29 wild fish were tagged and released from March 9, 2011, to May 20, 2011. The number of wild-origin fish collected was low with both gear types. Between March 7 and May 17, we deployed the Lampara seine 147 sets, and collected 21 wild yearling Chinook salmon. The Oneida Lake trap net was fished on 26 d and collected 22 wild yearling Chinook salmon we could use. The average size of tagged hatchery and wild fish was similar. The average fork lengths were 121.4 mm (range 98–152 mm) for hatchery fish and 120.6 mm (range 99–150 mm) for wild fish (table 1; note that one wild fish with a fork length of 215 mm was omitted from the size summary). The sizes of the wild fish from the two collection methods also were similar (table 2). The tag weight to body weight ratio based on the 0.53 g weight of the acoustic transmitter plus the PIT tag ranged from 1.6 to 6.0 percent with an average of 3.0 percent.

No hatchery fish died between collection and release, but 10 of the 43 wild fish collected (23 percent) died prior to release. One fish captured in the Lampara seine was released prior to tagging, and seven fish from the Oneida Lake trap were not tagged; three were rejected based on condition and released alive, and four died before surgery. There was a 5.0 percent (1 of 20) post-tagging mortality rate of fish collected in the Lampara seine and a 33.3 percent (5 of 15) post-tagging mortality rate of fish collected in the Oneida Lake trap.

Many of the wild fish were infected by a parasitic copepod. A total of 31 of the 41 wild fish examined had copepods present either on the gills (76 percent), at the insertion of the pectoral or pelvic fins, or a combination of these locations. One copepod was found on a hatchery fish (1 of 415; less than 1 percent). Samples of the copepods and 7 of the mortalities with copepods were sent to the U.S. Fish and Wildlife Service, Lower Columbia River Fish Health Center, in Willard, Washington. Five of the fish had no detectable levels of virus or bacteria tested for, but 2 fish tested positive for bacterial kidney disease (appendix A). The copepods examined by U.S. Fish and Wildlife Service staff were consistent with the genus *Salmincola* (Mary Peters, written commun., 2011).

Several observations were omitted prior to analysis. One wild fish with a fork length of 215 mm was omitted because it was more than 50 mm larger than any other fish captured and was likely not in the same year class as the others. Data from three hatchery fish and one wild fish that were never detected after release were omitted. Data from one wild fish and one hatchery fish that traveled

Table 1. Summary statistics of fork length (mm) and weight (g) of hatchery and wild juvenile Chinook salmon acoustic- and PIT-tagged during spring, Cougar Reservoir, Oregon, 2011.

[N, number of fish collected; SD, standard deviation]

Fish origin	Fork Length				Weight		
	N	Mean	SD	Range	Mean	SD	Range
Hatchery	415	121.4	7.3	98–152	17.9	3.2	9.3–32.3
Wild	28	120.6	12.1	99–150	17.3	5.5	8.8–33.5

Table 2. Summary statistics of fork length (mm) and weight (g) by the different collection methods used to capture wild Chinook salmon during the spring, Cougar Reservoir, Oregon, 2011.

[N, number of fish collected; SD, standard deviation]

Collection method	Fork Length				Weight		
	N	Mean	SD	Range	Mean	SD	Range
Lampara seine	19	120.8	12.3	99–150	17.3	5.7	8.8–33.3
Oneida Lake trap	9	120.1	12.5	100–138	17.2	5.4	9.5–25.3

continuously together near the temperature control tower and were suspected of being eaten by a predator were omitted. The environmental data from the 7 a.m. hour on May 25 were omitted because the data indicated that the discharge was 4,100 ft^3/s, which was at least 1,560 ft^3/s greater than the discharge in the adjacent hours. After omitting all these data, the analyses used 411 (415-4) hatchery fish and 26 (29-3) wild fish.

Environmental Conditions and Dam Operations

The dam operation differed before and after the reservoir was full. As the reservoir was being filled, the water elevation increased gradually and the depth of water over the top of the weir gates (head) ranged from 6.4 to 37.3 ft, with a median of 11.5 ft (fig. 5). The weir gates were operated so that the upper series of three gates were at similar elevations and controlled head. Discharge varied little during this period (range 400–3,160 ft^3/s, median 860 ft^3/s) except for a sharp increase and decrease in head and discharge during a week-long test discharge period in late April. After the reservoir was full, the head ranged from 5.0 to 37.0 ft, but it was usually operated at a much larger head than when the reservoir was filling, with a median of 20.7 ft from May 13, 2011, to August 3, 2011. The head increased sharply from 16.1 to 37.0 ft between 5 p.m. and 8 p.m. on May 13, 2011, at the end of reservoir filling period. Total discharge ranged from 850 to 2,620 ft^3/s with a median of 1,180 ft^3/s after the reservoir was full. Water elevation increased during the reservoir filling period and varied little after the reservoir was full, except that it began to lower in late June. Water temperature increased steadily until early July, with the highest rate of increase after mid-June 2011.

Vertical water temperature profiles at comparable depths were similar near the boat restricted zone and near the release site (fig. 6). A thermocline was present between approximately 10 and 30 ft in depth, depending on the date. The water temperature profiles from the two reservoir sites generally were similar to the data from the sensors at the temperature control tower.

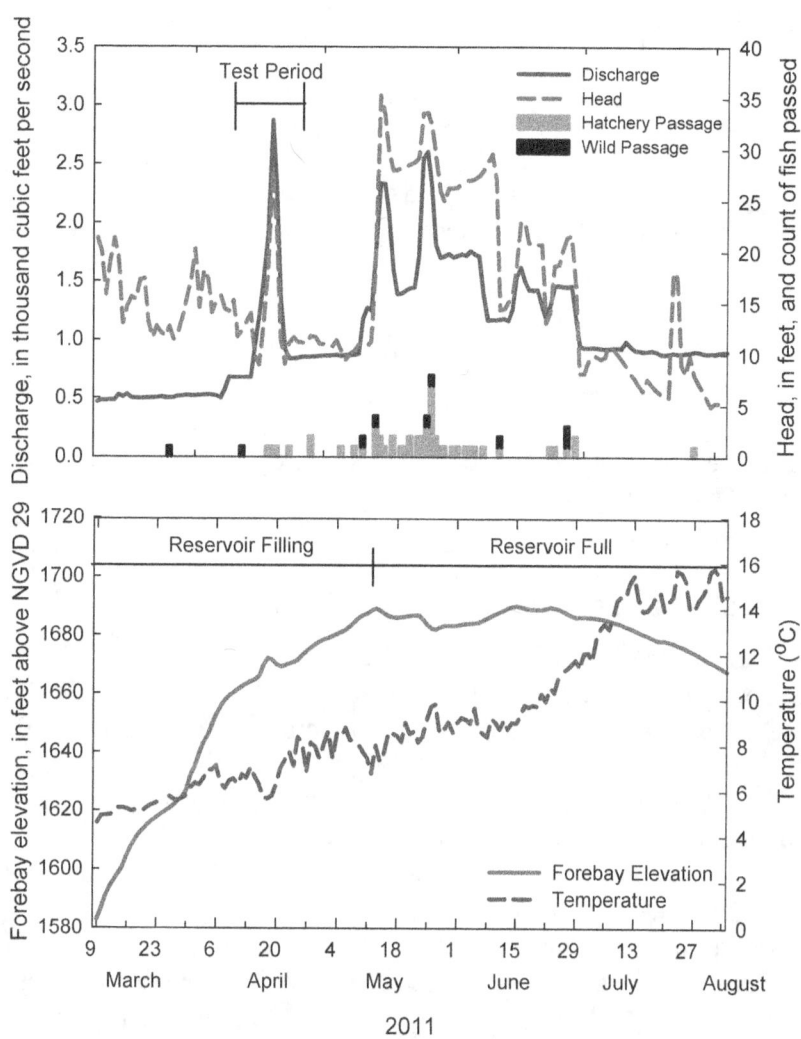

Figure 5. Graphs of total dam discharge and head above the weir gates (top) and forebay elevation and water temperature (bottom) at Cougar Dam, Oregon, 2011. Water temperature is the average of the top 13–19 feet of the water column near the temperature control tower. In addition, the top graph indicates dates of dam passage of wild and hatchery fish and test discharge periods, and the bottom graph indicates reservoir filling and reservoir full periods.

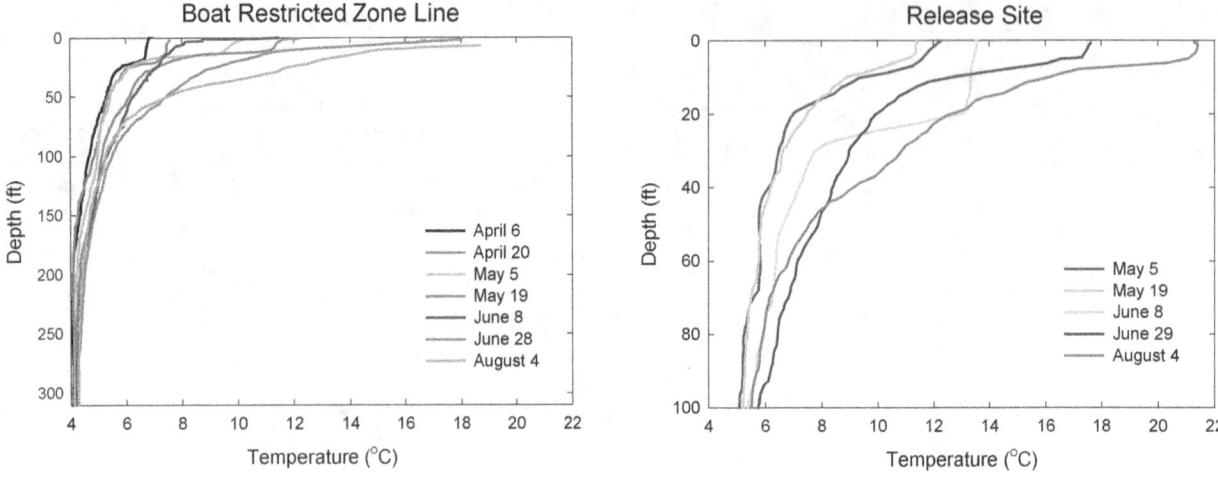

Figure 6. Vertical temperature profiles of Cougar Reservoir, Oregon, collected at the boat restricted zone and the fish release site from April 6 to August 4, 2011.

Dam Passage and Movements within the Reservoir

The operational life of the transmitters determined empirically was greater than expected. Transmitters in the tag-life study operated for a median of 110.7 d (range 27.5–127.5 d) and the 90th percentile of operational life was 118.5 d. The manufacturer's advertised tag life was 91 d. The 90th percentile of detections of tagged fish was 116.2 d after tag activation.

Most dam passage occurred at night. Only 6 of the 55 known passage events occurred during the day (fig. 7). We do not know the time of passage for one wild fish known to have passed after the acoustic transmitter stopped working (it was detected by the PIT system at Willamette Falls Dam on July 11, 2011, at 7:37 a.m.).

A total of 49 of the 411 hatchery fish and 7 of the 26 wild fish are known to have passed the dam, including the one wild fish that passed the dam after its acoustic tag stopped operating and was detected by the PIT system at Willamette Falls Dam (last acoustic transmitter data from this fish was received 100 d post-release). This represents a total dam passage rate of 11.9 percent for hatchery fish (95-percent confidence interval 8.4–15.5 percent), and 26.9 percent for wild fish (95-percent confidence interval 3.6–50.2 percent). More conservative estimates, based on the 91-d expected tag life, are 46 of 411 hatchery fish for a passage rate of 11.2 percent (95-percent confidence interval 7.8–14.6 percent), and 4 of 26 wild fish for a passage rate of 15.4 percent (95-percent confidence interval -1.0-31.8 percent) during the follow-up period.

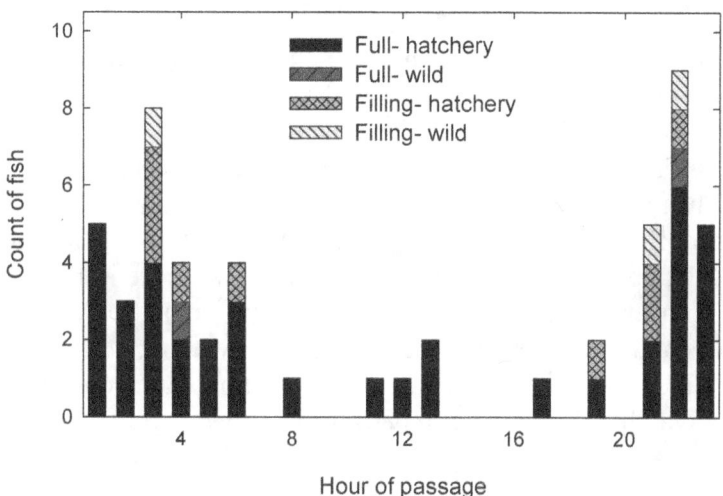

Figure 7. Hour of last detection of juvenile Chinook salmon with acoustic transmitters released during the spring at Cougar Dam, Oregon assigned dam passage, by rearing type and reservoir filling or full periods, 2011.

Travel Time from Release to the Temperature Control Tower and Release to Dam Passage

Travel times of the first trip from release to the temperature control tower were similar for hatchery and wild fish. Travel times ranged from 0.6 to 76.6 d for hatchery fish and from 3.3 to 36.4 d for wild fish, with medians of 9.7 and 9.1 d for hatchery and wild fish, respectively (fig. 8). A total of 342 hatchery fish and 18 wild fish were detected near the temperature control tower.

The times from release to dam passage also were similar for hatchery and wild fish. The median times were 34.5 d for hatchery fish and 34.2 d for wild fish. Time from release to dam passage ranged from 2.5 to 94.6 d for hatchery fish and 17.2 to 110.2 d for wild fish. A total of 49 hatchery fish and 6 wild fish were detected passing the dam. As previously mentioned, one additional wild fish is known to have passed the dam after the acoustic transmitter stopped operating, because it was detected at the PIT system at Willamette Falls Dam on July 11, 2011, at 7:37 a.m.

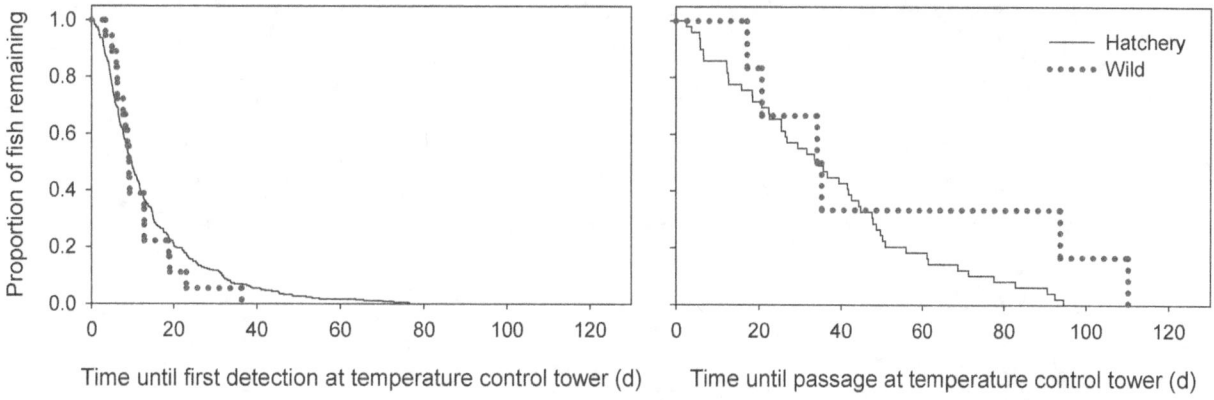

Figure 8. Time (days) from release to first detection at the temperature control tower (left) and time (days) from release to passage (right) for hatchery (solid line) and wild (dotted line) juvenile Chinook salmon release during the spring at Cougar Dam, Oregon, 2011.

Probability of Presence near the Temperature Control Tower

The probabilities of presence at each array and at the temperature control tower were based on model-averaged estimates from a suite of models. The nine models included four models of presence probability, each with two models of detection probability (models 1 and 2 in table 3), and one model of common values across factors (table 4). Five of the nine models received a total of nearly 96 percent of the model weights. The model-averaged detection probabilities ranged from 0.959 (SE 0.012) to 1.000 (SE 0.000) for hatchery fish, and from 0.961 (SE 0.048) to 1.000 (SE 0.000) for wild fish.

The probability of being present decreased as the distance from the release site increased (fig. 9). The data and models moderately supported differences between hatchery and wild fish, as indicated by the QAICc differences of about 4 between models with and without origin as a factor (table 4). The estimated cumulative probability of fish presence at the temperature control tower at least once is 0.835 (SE 0.023) for hatchery fish and 0.665 (SE 0.086) for wild fish.

Table 3. Suite of models of detection probabilities for the analysis of presence probabilities, Cougar Dam, Oregon, 2011.

[Models of detection probability (P) include combinations of fish origin (hatchery, wild), array, and a common value fitted to all combinations of origin and array (.). All models shared a common presence probability model of a multiplicative combination of origin and array. Num. Par is number of parameters and + indicates an additive effect. A $\hat{c}$ value of 1.551 was applied to the data]

Model	QAICc	Delta QAICc	QAICc Weights	Model Likelihood	Num. Par	QDeviance
1 P(origin+array)	640.466	0.000	0.513	1.000	14	24.454
2 P(array)	640.587	0.121	0.483	0.941	13	26.598
3 P(origin)	650.714	10.248	0.003	0.006	10	42.786
4 P(.)	652.473	12.008	0.001	0.003	11	42.527

Table 4. Suite of models used in estimation of presence probabilities, Cougar Dam, Oregon, 2011.

[Models of presence probability (M) include combinations of fish origin (hatchery, wild), array, and a common value fitted to all combinations of origin and array (.). Num. Par is number of parameters, + indicates an additive effect, and * indicates a multiplicative effect. A $\hat{c}$ value of 1.551 was applied to the data]

Model	QAICc	Delta QAICc	QAICc Weights	Model Likelihood	Num. Par	QDeviance
1 M(origin+array), P(origin+array)	636.267	0.000	0.405	1.000	11	26.321
2 M(origin+array), P(array)	636.338	0.070	0.391	0.966	10	28.410
3 M(array), P(array)	639.886	3.618	0.066	0.164	9	33.974
4 M(origin*array), P(origin+array)	640.466	4.198	0.050	0.123	14	24.454
5 M(origin*array), P(array)	640.587	4.320	0.047	0.115	13	26.598
6 M(origin), P(array)	642.772	6.505	0.016	0.039	6	42.901
7 M(.), P(origin+array)	643.658	7.391	0.010	0.025	6	43.787
8 M(.), P(array)	643.819	7.551	0.009	0.023	5	45.958
9 M(origin), P(origin+array)	644.490	8.223	0.007	0.016	7	42.608

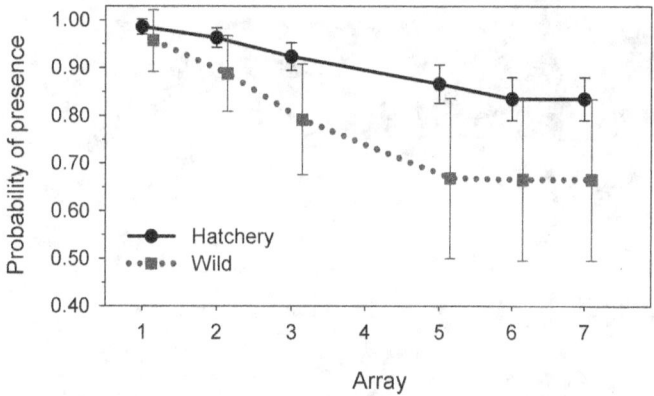

Figure 9. Cumulative probabilities (± 95-percent confidence interval) of being present at least once at reservoir arrays 1, 2, 3, and 5, and at arrays 6 and 7 near the temperature control tower, Cougar Dam, Oregon, 2011. Array 4 in the eastern arm of the reservoir was not used in this analysis because fish can migrate to the temperature control tower without passing that location.

Fish Depths near the Temperature Control Tower

Fish depths were estimated from three-dimensional positions of fish within 74 m of the face of the temperature control tower. An example of one 24-hour period of these data is shown in figure 10. Depths of hatchery fish were slightly greater during the day than during the night. Data from the few wild fish available were too variable to determine patterns (fig. 11). Hourly data points are averages of the average hourly depths of 130–218 hatchery fish and 3–11 wild fish. Hourly average depths ranged from 2.2 to 4.9 m for hatchery fish and 0.6 to 9.6 m for wild fish. The mean depths over all times were 3.6 m for hatchery fish and 3.4 m for wild fish.

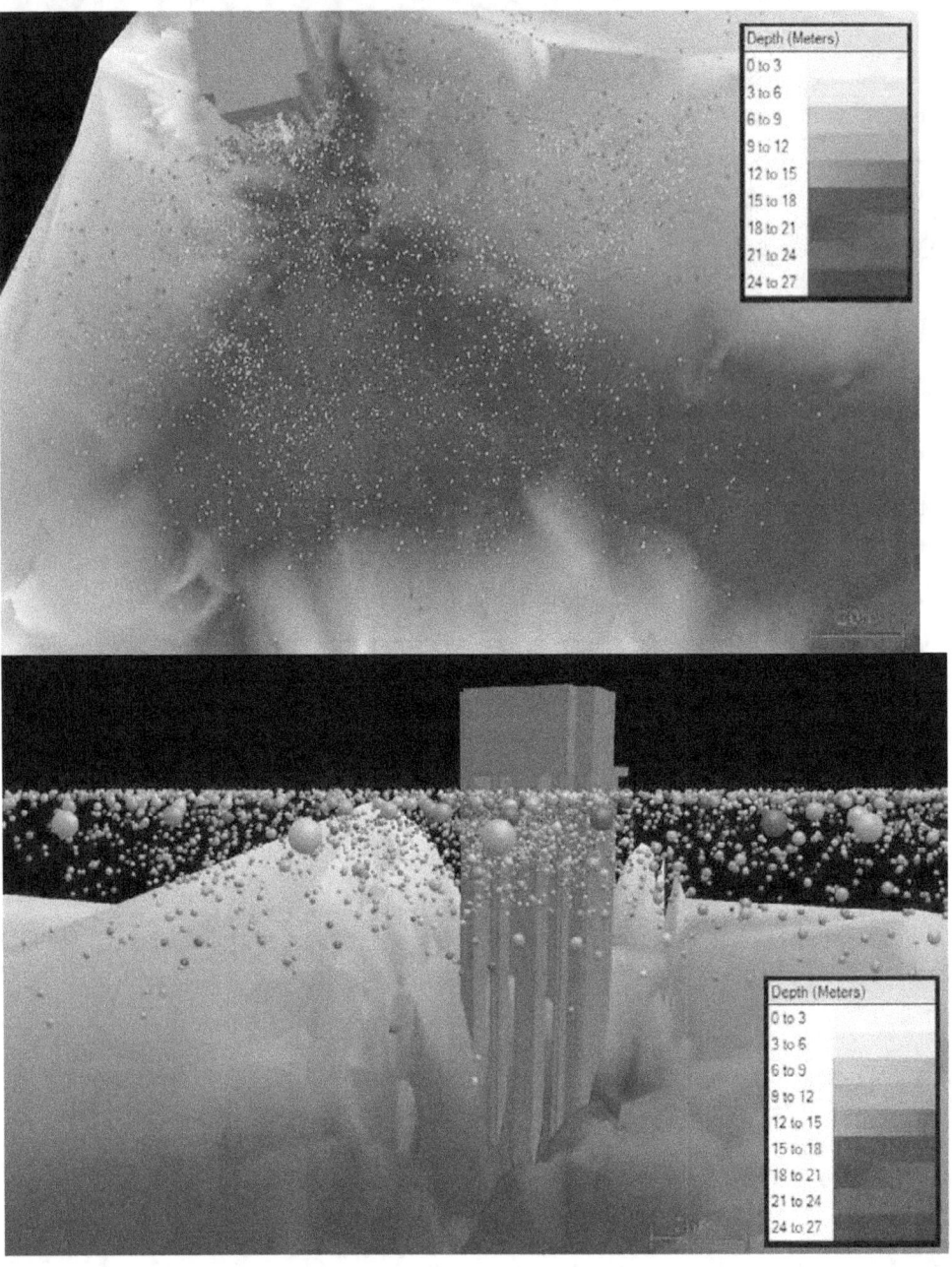

Figure 10. Three-dimensional fish position estimates from tagged fish near the temperature control tower at Cougar Dam, Oregon, 2011. The data shown are from the 24-period beginning June 29 at 6 a.m. The top image is an aerial view, and the bottom image is a cross-sectional view. Symbol colors indicate individual fish, and their relative sizes as spheres in the bottom image represents distance from the viewer (larger is closer). Legend is for bathymetry, and scale is relative to depth at the temperature control tower.

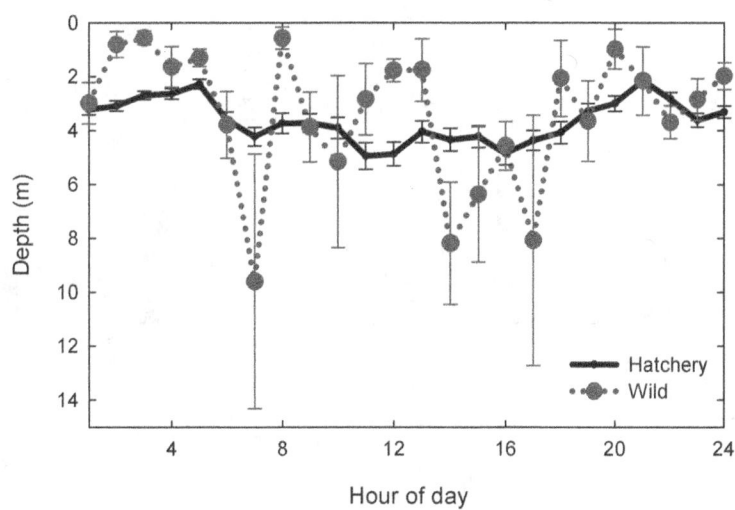

Figure 11. Least-squares mean depths (± 1 SE) of hatchery (solid line) and wild (dotted line) yearling Chinook salmon tagged with acoustic transmitters during the spring, Cougar Dam, Oregon, 2011. Data are the means of the mean depth of each fish in the zone of inference rounded to the nearest hour. Each point comprises data from 130 to 218 hatchery fish or 3 to 11 wild fish.

Movement Probabilities within the Reservoir

Results of analyses of transition probabilities between arrays in the reservoir indicate that fish movements were directional. Transition probabilities of hatchery and wild fish were estimated for 14 combinations of movements between adjacent reservoir arrays. Comparisons of models of the hypothesis that transition probabilities were a first-order Markov chain (random movement) or that transition probabilities depend on where a fish came from (a second-order Markov chain) indicate that, in all but 2 of the 32 possible cases, the second-order chain was supported. This indicates a high degree of directionality in fish movements within the reservoir. For example, there was a higher probability that both hatchery and wild fish moved downstream from array 1 to array 2 and then to array 3 (60–62 percent) than fish that moved downstream from array 1 to array 2 and then swam back upstream to array 1 (38–40 percent) (figs. 12 and 13). These results are consistent with movement patterns of fish within the reservoir, as shown for representative fish in figure 14. The exception to the directional movements occurred when fish moved from the eastern arm of the reservoir (array 4), in which case they were equally likely to move upstream or downstream. Fish near the log boom at the boat restricted zone were much more likely to swim to array 7 at the temperature control tower (73–74 percent) than they were to swim upstream. They also were more likely to swim from the tower upstream to the forebay line and then turn back downstream and swim to the tower (60–65 percent) than they were to swim from the tower to the forebay line and then proceed farther upstream. In the 4,703 hatchery fish movements from array 5 to array 7, they passed the dam 1.04 percent of the time, while out of 226 similar movements for wild fish, 3.10 percent passed the dam.

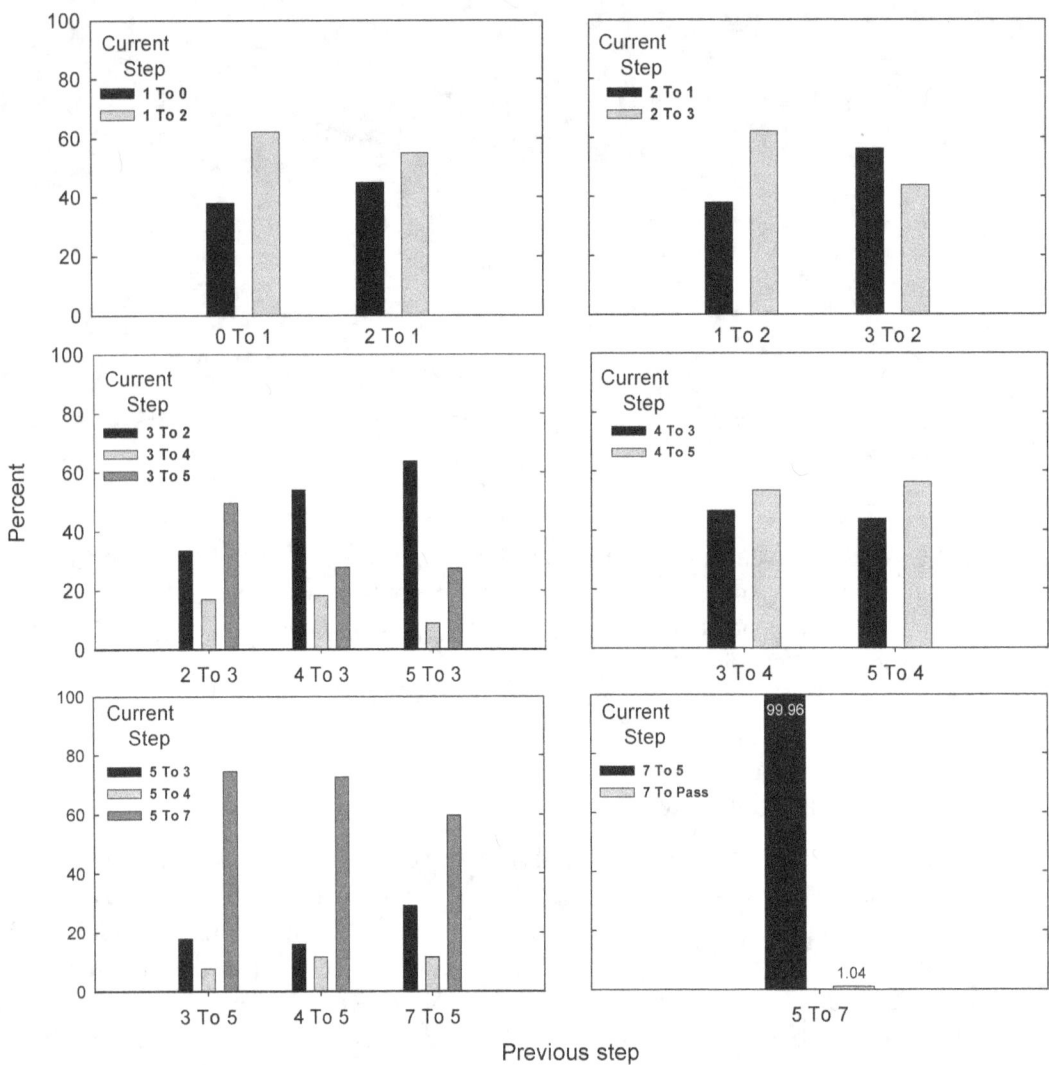

Figure 12. Transition probabilities of hatchery fish released during the spring, Cougar Dam, Oregon, 2011. Bars indicate probabilities of moving from one array to an adjacent array (current step) based on the previous movement (previous step).

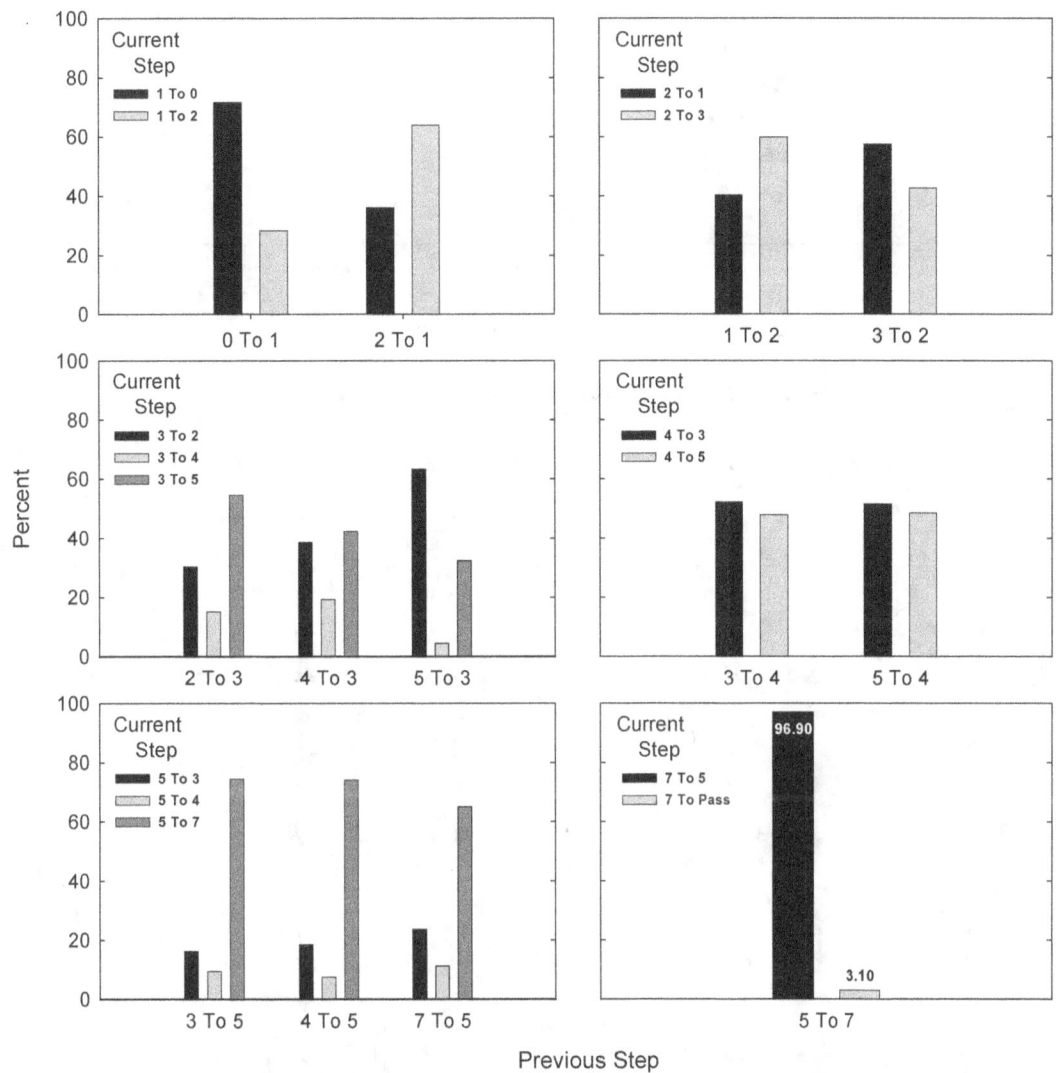

Figure 13. Transition probabilities of wild fish released in the spring, Cougar Dam, Oregon, 2011. Bars indicate probabilities of moving from one array to an adjacent array (current step) based on based on the previous movement (previous step).

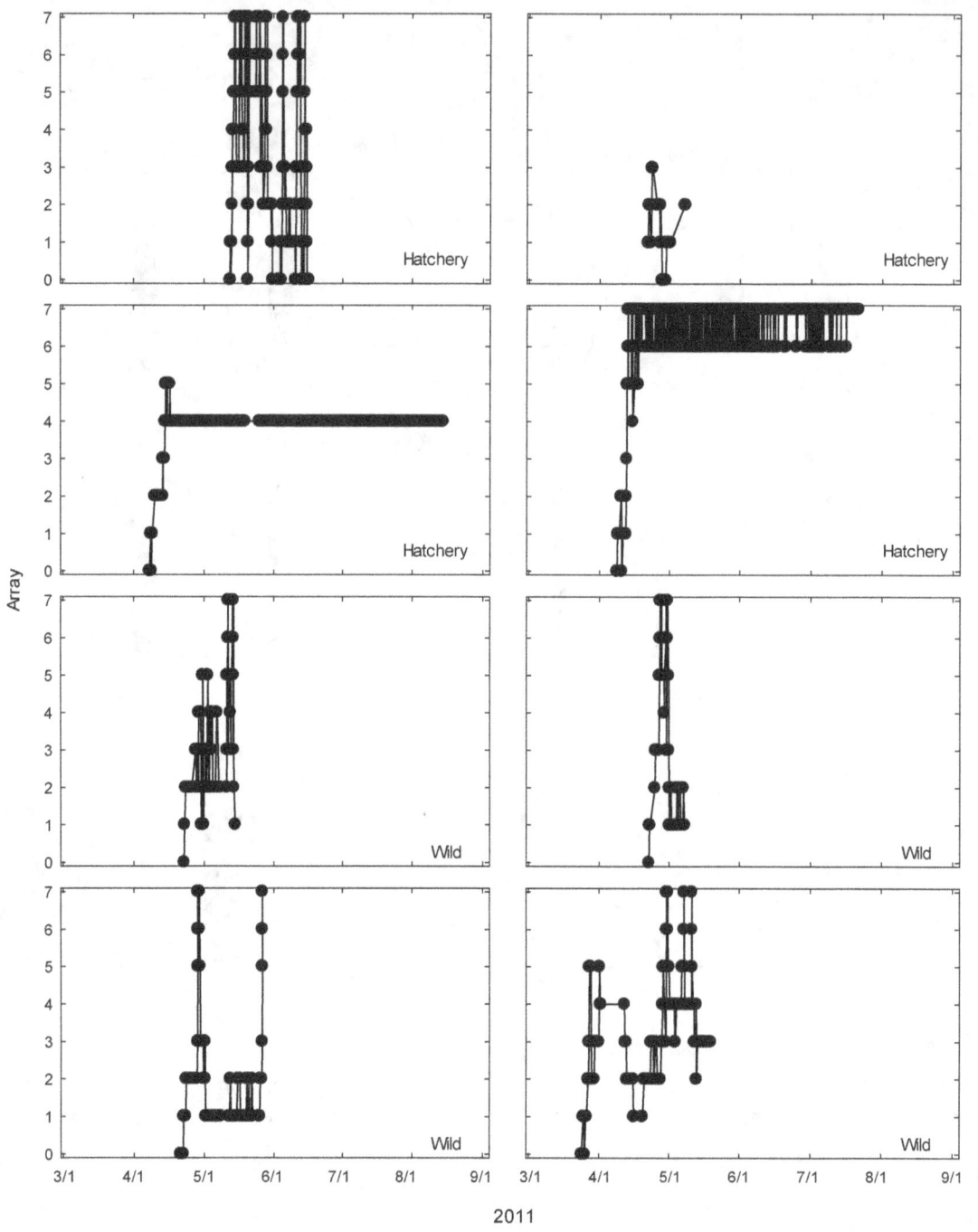

Figure 14. Graph of movements of several randomly selected fish released in the spring showing directionality in Cougar Reservoir, Oregon, 2011.

Fish Behavior during the Reservoir Filling Period

Three of the 18 tagged wild fish detected within about 100 m of the temperature control tower (zone 6) during the reservoir filling period passed the dam. All three fish passed at night. Individual wild fish were in zone 6 from 2 to 11 times with a median of 3.5 times per fish, spending a cumulative time ranging from 1.0 h to 7.7 d, with a median of 29.4 h. Tagged wild fish spent from less than 1 min to 82.4 h during each visit in zone 6, with a median of 2.4 h per visit.

A total of 9 of the 232 tagged hatchery fish detected within about 100 m of the temperature control tower (zone 6) during the reservoir filling period passed the dam. Seven of the fish passed at night and two passed during the day. Individual hatchery fish spent a cumulative time of 0.2 to 24.2 d in zone 6, with a median of 25.8 h per fish. Individual fish made 1–87 trips into the zone, with a median of 4 trips per fish. Tagged hatchery fish spent from less than 1 min to 22.5 d during each visit in zone 6, with a median of 0.9 h per visit.

Fish Behavior After the Reservoir Was Full

Three of the eight tagged wild fish detected within about 100 m from the temperature control tower (zone 6) after the reservoir was full passed the dam. All three passed at night. Recall that three wild fish passed prior to the reservoir being full. Individual wild fish were in zone 6 from 1 to 36 times with a median of 12 times per fish, spending a cumulative time ranging from 0.2 h to 113.7 d there, with a median of 39.1 h. Tagged wild fish spent from 0.6 min to 113.7 d during each visit in zone 6, with a median of 1.6 h per visit.

A total of 40 of the 257 tagged hatchery fish detected within about 100 m from the temperature control tower (zone 6) after the reservoir was full passed the dam. Nine hatchery fish passed during the day and 31 passed at night. Tagged hatchery fish spent a cumulative time in zone 6 ranging from 0.2 h to 128.0 d, with a median of 40.9 h per fish. Individual fish made 1–82 trips into the zone, with a median of 11 trips per fish. Tagged hatchery fish spent from 0.3 min to 128.0 d during each visit in zone 6, with a median of 2.2 h per visit.

Fish Behavior During the Spring Test Discharge Period

There were not sufficient numbers of fish passing the dam during the spring test discharge period to warrant statistical analysis. Four hatchery fish and one wild fish passed the dam during the spring discharge test period. All fish passed the dam at night. Recall that, for the purpose of analysis, the spring test period includes pre- and post-test periods each equal to 50 percent of the duration of the test discharge period (the 267 h from April 15 at 6 a.m. to April 21 at 2 p.m.). Six wild fish and 84 hatchery fish were detected in zone 6 during this period. Individual wild fish were in zone 6 from 1 to 29 times with a median of 3.5 times per fish. Individual hatchery fish made 1–49 trips into the zone, with a median of 3 trips per fish.

Effects of Dam Discharge and Diurnal Period on Dam Passage

Data from three-dimensional fish positions were used to estimate the effects of the discharge and diurnal period on rates of dam passage. Recall that the period of this data was from April 21, 2011, at 4 p.m. to August 3, 2011, at 12 p.m., the end of the analysis period covered in this report.

Dam passage rates were affected by discharge and diel period. The lack of passage events in some combinations of discharge and diel period suggested that dividing the data into discharge bins rather than using discharge as a continuous covariate would be useful. The discharge ranges for each bin were chosen to capture steps present in the data, but were otherwise arbitrary.

The rate of dam passage did not increase with discharge until the discharge bin had a flow rate of at least 1,200 ft^3/s. Rates of dam passage were similar when discharge was in the bin of 900 to less than 1,200 ft^3/s, and the bin of less than 900 ft^3/s (the reference bin used for analysis). The statistical significance of discharge increased as the flow rate in the discharge bin increased. For example, for fish within 74 m of the temperature control tower, the P-value of the 900 to less than 1,200 ft^3/s bin was 0.2546, the P-value of 1,200 to less than 1,800 ft^3/s bin was 0.0957, and the P-value of 1,800-ft^3/s-or-greater bin was less than 0.0001 (table 5). The hazard ratios also increased as the flow rate of the discharge bin increased, meaning that the difference in rate of dam passage increased relative to the flow rate of the reference bin (900 ft^3/s). The rate of dam passage of fish within 74 m of the tower when discharge was 1,200 to less than 1,800 ft^3/s was 2.278 times the rate of the reference range. When discharge was 1,800 ft^3/s or greater, the passage rate was 7.693 times greater than the reference range. This pattern continued as the data were restricted to fish within smaller distances from the tower, with the rates of dam passage relative to the reference discharge increasing as the distance from the dam was decreased. The rate of dam passage of fish within 14 m of the tower when discharge was 1,800 ft^3/s or greater was more than 23 times the rate at the reference discharge of 900 ft^3/s. Data from the zone within 4 m of the face of the temperature control tower were not used separately in analyses because tagged fish could traverse the zone without being detected as a result of the slow pulse rate interval of the transmitters.

The rate of dam passage was higher during the night than during the day. The rate of dam passage ranged from 4.463 to 7.830 times higher at night than during the day, depending on the distance from the dam. The effect increased as distance from the dam decreased.

Table 5. Regression coefficients from analysis of the effects of discharge and diel period on the rate of dam passage of fish within 74 meters of the face of the temperature control tower, Cougar Dam, Oregon, 2011.

[Results are based on analysis of dam passage of tagged fish within four distances (in meters) from the temperature control tower, estimated from three-dimensional fish positions. Pr > ChiSq = probability of a larger Chi-Square value under the hypothesis that the estimate = 0, < is less than. Variables represent ranges of dam discharge bins in ft^3/s (1,800 or more, 1,200 to < 1,800, 900 to < 1,200) and diel period (Diel, 0 = day, 1 = night). Hazard ratios of variables describing discharge are relative to dam passage rates during discharge of less than 900 ft^3/s. "na" indicates that no fish passed during that discharge range. Each row is based on one degree of freedom]

Distance from tower (m)	Variable	Parameter estimate	Standard error	Chi-square	Pr > ChiSq	Hazard ratio	95-percent hazard ratio confidence limits	
< 74	1,800 or more	2.0403	0.4971	16.8484	< 0.0001	7.693	2.904	20.378
	1,200 <1,800	0.8231	0.4940	2.7762	0.0957	2.278	0.865	5.998
	900 <1,200	-1.2550	1.1015	1.2981	0.2546	0.285	0.033	2.469
	Diel	1.4958	0.3877	14.8845	0.0001	4.463	2.087	9.542
< 54	1,800 or more	2.2826	0.5531	17.0306	< 0.0001	9.802	3.315	28.983
	1,200<1,800	1.0267	0.5422	3.5850	0.0583	2.792	0.965	8.080
	900 <1,200	-1.1517	1.1181	1.0610	0.3030	0.316	0.035	2.829
	Diel	1.7105	0.3722	21.1221	< 0.0001	5.532	2.667	11.472
< 34	1,800 or more	2.7640	0.5469	25.5406	< 0.0001	15.863	5.431	46.337
	1,200 <1,800	1.3194	0.5310	6.1746	0.0130	3.741	1.321	10.591
	900 <1,200	na	na	na	na	na	na	na
	Diel	1.7444	0.3718	22.0148	< 0.0001	5.722	2.761	11.858
< 14	1,800 or more	3.1457	0.6267	25.1921	< 0.0001	23.236	6.803	79.365
	1,200 <1,800	1.7670	0.6118	8.3429	0.0039	5.853	1.765	19.415
	900 <1,200	na	na	na	na	na	na	na
	Diel	2.0580	0.3929	27.4346	< 0.0001	7.830	3.625	16.912

Discussion

Tagged juvenile Chinook salmon in Cougar Reservoir moved about the reservoir in a directed manner and were often present near the dam outlet, but conditions conducive to dam passage rarely were present. Most fish of hatchery or wild origin were within at least 100 m of the outlet at the temperature control tower at least once, but few had passed the dam by August 3, 2011. The rate of dam passage of fish near the temperature control tower was affected by dam discharge and diel period. The rates of dam passage did not change significantly until the dam discharge was at least 1,200 ft^3/s; however, the discharge bins were chosen arbitrarily and the true threshold may differ from that value. The threshold evident in the data examined was common among datasets representing fish within various distances of the temperature control tower, ranging from 14 to 74 m. Dam passage rate also was much greater during the night than during the day, with the effect more pronounced as fish were closer to the dam. Additional data are needed to determine more definitively the factors affecting dam passage rate and the relations between those factors. The data used in this report represent dam operations occurring during the spring and summer, during which period the reservoir was filling or full.

Conditions likely will differ as the reservoir elevation is reduced in preparation for storage to avert flooding downstream in winter.

Dam passage at other dams also is predominantly during the night when passage routes are not readily used. Lower Granite and Little Goose Dams on the Snake River in Washington State are examples of this pattern. Prior to the installation of spillway weirs at these sites, juvenile salmonid passage was often greater at night (Plumb and others, 2002; Perry and others, 2007). Even after a spillway weir was present at Little Goose Dam in 2009, the passage rates of juvenile Chinook salmon through the juvenile bypass system were greater at night than during the day (Beeman and others, 2010). The entrances of the juvenile bypass systems at Lower Granite and Little Goose Dams are much deeper than the entrances of the spillway weirs. Perry and others (2007) also reported that at Little Goose Dam, during periods without water passing through the Tainter gates at the spillway, it was common for juvenile salmonids to reach the dam and return upstream several times prior to passage. This is similar to the behaviors of fish in Cougar Reservoir, where fish traveled repeatedly from the release site near the head of the reservoir to the dam outlet and back again.

It is useful to consider fish passage at barriers in terms of the component processes of guidance, attraction, and passage (Castro-Santos and Haro, 2010). Guidance is the process of getting fish near enough to the desired passage route that they can detect the existence of the route. Attraction is the process of getting fish close enough to the route that they will enter it, conditional on guidance. Passage is the process of retaining fish within a route once they enter it to result in passage rather than rejection, conditional on attraction. Safe passage through the route, or "conveyance", also is an important consideration (see Sweeney and others, 2007), but may be of secondary importance if passage is not achieved (there was no evaluation of the survival of tagged fish passing the dam in this study). The data we examined indicate that fish guidance to within about 100 m of the dam (zone 6) outlet occurred often, but that fish passed the dam at a low rate. Data analysis based on fish position estimates near the temperature control tower suggests guidance and attraction were present, but passage was lacking.

There are many similarities in results from hatchery and wild yearling Chinook salmon, but little data from wild fish were available for analysis. The probability of presence near the temperature control tower was slightly lower for wild fish than hatchery fish, but the estimates for wild fish were imprecise because of the small sample size. The lower probability of presence at the tower for wild fish also may have been affected by fish condition prior to tagging, since pre- and post-tagging mortalities of wild fish were higher than for hatchery fish. The water depths of the two groups were similar when within 74 m of the temperature control tower, although the estimates for wild fish are imprecise due to the small sample size. The passage rates of the two groups also are similar, although once again the estimate for wild fish is imprecise. A comprehensive comparison of hatchery and wild fish will require more data from wild fish.

Data from fish positions near the temperature control tower can be analyzed further and should be compared to results of numerical models of water velocities near the tower. The depths of fish near the tower are similar to the water depth over the weir gates, but passage rates are low. Examining predicted water velocities and vectors along with fish paths may help determine the water velocities required to entrain juvenile Chinook salmon, which will be needed for the design of a successful juvenile fish collection device. The COE has already developed a computational fluid dynamics model of the reservoir that could be used for this purpose. The tagged fish commonly were present throughout the 74-m-radius semicircular area upstream from the tower (fig. 4) used in the current analysis.

This report is an interim summary of the data collected as of August 3, 2011, for use by fishery managers and other interested parties in considering future research needs. Data from the fish released during spring 2011 were still being collected in August 2011. Based on the data and models examined, there is little evidence to suggest a difference between hatchery and wild yearling Chinook salmon in migration within the reservoir, probability of presence at the temperature control tower, or percentage of fish passing the dam. However, more data from wild fish are needed to better evaluate these questions. Tagged fish were commonly moving throughout the reservoir and were often near the face of the temperature control tower. The rate of dam passage was positively related to dam discharge rate, but little change in dam passage rate occurred at discharge rates of less than 1,200 ft^3/s. Most dam passage occurred at night.

Acknowledgments

Many people assisted with this study. The State of Oregon staff at the McKenzie River Fish Hatchery provided study fish and holding space, and were gracious in allowing us to use their facility. The staff at Cougar Dam assisted us in many aspects of logistics at the site. Fred Monzyk and his staff of the Oregon Department of Fish and Wildlife provided wild fish from their Oneida Lake trap. Ty Hatton, Matt Sholtis, Dana Shurtleff, and Nick Swyers of the U.S. Geological Survey assisted with field work and data analysis. Dave Griffith, Scott Fielding, and Rich Piaskowski of the U.S. Army Corps of Engineers, Portland District, arranged contracts and provided helpful information and coordination for the study. The report was improved after review by Noah Adams of the U.S. Geological Survey and Tom Friesen of the Oregon Department of Fish and Wildlife. Funding for this project was provided by the U.S. Army Corps of Engineers, Portland District, Contract W66QKZ03023085.

References Cited

Allison, P.D., 1995, Survival analysis using SAS®—A practical guide: Cary, N.C., SAS Institute Inc., 292 p.

Bhat, U.N., and Miller, G.K., 2002, Elements of applied stochastic processes: Hoboken, N.J., John Wiley and Sons, 461 p.

Beeman, J.W., Braatz, A.C., Hansel, H.C., Fielding, S.D., Haner, P.V., Hansen, G.S., Shurtleff, D.J., Sprando, J.M., and Rondorf, D.W., 2010, Approach, passage, and survival of juvenile salmonids at Little Goose Dam, Washington: Post-construction evaluation of a temporary spillway weir, 2009: U.S. Geological Survey Open-File Report 2010-1224, 100 p. Available at *http://pubs.er.usgs.gov/publication/ofr20101224.*

Burnham, K.P., and Anderson, D.R., 2002, Model selection and multimodel inference—A practical information-theoretic approach: New York, Springer-Verlag, 488 p.

Castro-Santos, T., and Haro, A., 2003, Quantifying migratory delay—A new application of survival analysis methods: Canadian Journal of Fisheries and Aquatic Sciences, v. 60, p. 986–996.

Castro-Santos, T., and Haro, A., 2010, Fish guidance and passage at barriers *in* Domenici, P., and Kapoor, B.G., eds., Fish locomotion—An eco-ethological perspective: Enfield, N.H., Science Publishers, p. 62–89.

Cormack, R.M., 1964, Estimates of survival from the sighting of marked animals: Biometrika, v. 51, no. 3/4, p. 429–438.

Hosmer, D.W., and Lemeshow, S., 1999, Applied survival analysis: Regression modeling of time to event data: New York, John Wiley and Sons, Inc., 386 p.

Johnson, G.E., Hedgepeth, J.B., Skalski, J.R., and Giorgi, A.E., 2004, A Markov chain analysis of fish movements to determine entrainment zones: Fisheries Research, v. 69, p. 349–358.

Jolly, G.M., 1965, Explicit estimates from capture-recapture data with both death and immigration-stochastic model: Biometrika, v. 52, no. 1/2, p. 225–247.

National Oceanic and Atmospheric Administration, 2008, Biological Opinion and Magnuson-Stevens Fishery Conservation and Management Act essential fish habitat consultation—Willamette River Basin Flood Control Project: Endangered Species Act Section 7(a)(2) Consultation, NOAA Fisheries Log No. FINWRl2000/02117, June 11, 2008, accessed April 24, 2012, at *https://pcts.nmfs.noaa.gov/pls/pcts-pub/pcts_upload.summary_list_biop?p_id=26588.*

Perry, R.W., Novick, M.S., Braatz, A.C., Kock, T.J., Pope, A.C., Shurtleff, D.J., Lampson, S.N., Burns, R.K., Adams, N.S., and Rondorf, D.W., 2007, Survival and migration behavior of juvenile salmonids at Little Goose Dam, 2005: Final report of research by the U. S. Geological Survey to the U.S. Army Corps of Engineers, Walla Walla District, Contract W68SBV50568470, Walla Walla, Wash., 154 p.

Plumb, J.M., Novick, M.S., Adams, N.S., and Rondorf, D.W., 2002, Behavior of radio-tagged juvenile Chinook salmon and steelhead in the forebay of Lower Granite Dam relative to the 2000 surface bypass and behavioral guidance structure tests: Annual report by the U. S. Geological Survey to the U.S. Army Corps of Engineers, Contract E-86930151, Walla Walla, Wash., 61 p.

Seber, G.A.F., 1965, A note on the multiple-recapture census: Biometrika, v. 52, no. 1/2, p. 249–259.

Seber, G.A.F., 1982, The estimation of animal abundance and related parameters: New York, Macmillan, 654 p.

Surgical Protocols Steering Committee, 2011, Surgical protocols for implanting JSATS transmitters into juvenile salmonids for studies conducted for the U.S. Army Corps of Engineers: Report prepared by Surgical Protocols Steering Committee for U.S. Army Corps of Engineers, Portland, Oreg.

Sweeney, C.E., Giorgi, A.E., Johnson, G.E., Hall, R., and Miller, M., 2007, Surface bypass program comprehensive review report: ENSR Corporation document no. 09000-399-0409, 494 p.

Titzler, P.S., McMichael, G.A., and Carter, J.A., 2010, Autonomous acoustic receiver deployment and mooring techniques for use in large rivers and estuaries: North American Journal of Fisheries Management, v. 30, p. 853–859.

Weiland, M.A., Ploskey, G.R., Hughes, J.S., Deng, Z., Fu, T., Monter, T.J., Johnson, G.E., Khan, F., Wilberding, M.C., Cushing, A.W., Zimmerman, S.A., Faber, D.M., Durham, R.E., Townsend, R.L., Skalski, J.R., Kim, J., Fischer, E.S., and Meyer, M.M., 2009, Acoustic telemetry evaluation of juvenile salmonid passage and survival at John Day Dam with emphasis on the prototype surface flow outlet, 2008: Pacific Northwest National Laboratory, Report PNNL-18890, Richland, Wash., 259 p.

White, G.C., and Burnham, K.P., 1999, Program MARK—survival estimation from populations of marked animals: Bird Study, v. 46 (supplement), p. 120–138.

Appendix A. Fish health reports of yearling Chinook salmon submitted during spring and summer 2011 from Cougar Reservoir, Oregon.

U.S. FISH & WILDLIFE SERVICE
LOWER COLUMBIA RIVER FISH HEALTH CENTER
201 Oklahoma Road
Willard, WA 98605
Phone: 509-538-2400
Fax: 509-538-2404

FISH HEALTH REPORT 2011

FISH SOURCE	FISH EXAMINED
Location: Cougar Reservoir **County:** Lane **Contact Person:** John Beeman **Affiliation:** USGS **Phone:** (509) 538-2299	**Species:** Spring Chinook salmon **Age:** Yearlings **CHN:** W11-081 **Number of fish:** 4 **Date Sampled:** 5/18/2011

DISEASE AGENT [1]	SAMPLE SIZE	RESULTS	COMMENTS
IPNV	4	not detected	EPC and CHSE-214 cells
IHNV	4	not detected	EPC and CHSE-214 cells
VHS	4	not detected	EPC and CHSE-214 cells
SVCV	-	not tested	EPC and FHM cells
AS	4	not detected	BHIA medium
YR	4	not detected	BHIA medium
ESC	4	not detected	BHIA medium
BCD	4	not detected	TYES medium
CD	4	not detected	TYES medium
RS	1	not detected	ELISA
WD	4	not detected	Pepsin/Trypsin Digest
Comments	Frayed fins. All fish with *Salmincola*, one fish heavy infestation.		

[1] **IPNV** Infectious Pancreatic Necrosis Virus, **IHNV** Infectious Hematopoietic Necrosis Virus, **VHS** Viral Hemorrhagic Septicemia Virus, **SVCV** Spring Viremia of Carp Virus, **AS** Furunculosis (*Aeromonas salmonicida*), **YR** Enteric Redmouth (*Yersinia ruckeri*), **ESC** Emphysematous Putrefactive Disease (*Edwardsiella ictaluri*), **BCD** Coldwater Disease (*Flavobacterium psychrophilum*), **CD** Columnaris (*Flavobacterium columnare*), **RS** BKD (*Renibacterium salmoninarum*), **WD** Whirling Disease (*Myxobolus cerebralis*), **CS** Salmonid Ceratomyxosis (*Ceratomyxa shasta*).

U.S. FISH & WILDLIFE SERVICE
LOWER COLUMBIA RIVER FISH HEALTH CENTER
201 Oklahoma Road
Willard, WA 98605
Phone: 509-538-2400
Fax: 509-538-2404

FISH HEALTH REPORT 2011

FISH SOURCE	FISH EXAMINED
Location: Cougar Reservoir **County:** Lane **Contact Person:** John Beeman **Affiliation:** USGS **Phone:** (509) 538-2299	**Species:** Spring Chinook salmon **Age:** Yearlings **CHN:** W11-082 **Number of fish:** 3 **Date Sampled:** 5/20/2011

DISEASE AGENT [1]	SAMPLE SIZE	RESULTS	COMMENTS
IPNV	3	not detected	EPC and CHSE-214 cells
IHNV	3	not detected	EPC and CHSE-214 cells
VHS	3	not detected	EPC and CHSE-214 cells
SVCV	-	not tested	EPC and FHM cells
AS	3	not detected	BHIA medium
YR	3	not detected	BHIA medium
ESC	3	not detected	BHIA medium
BCD	3	not detected	TYES medium
CD	3	not detected	TYES medium
RS	3	**Positive**	+2/3 detected by ELISA, confirmed by PCR
WD	3	not detected	Pepsin/Trypsin Digest
Comments	Frayed fins, descaling. Gills with lots of excess mucus. All fish with *Salmincola*, one fish heavy infestation, other two fish with moderate infections. No food in stomachs and intestines.		

[1] **IPNV** Infectious Pancreatic Necrosis Virus, **IHNV** Infectious Hematopoietic Necrosis Virus, **VHS** Viral Hemorrhagic Septicemia Virus, **SVCV** Spring Viremia of Carp Virus, **AS** Furunculosis (*Aeromonas salmonicida*), **YR** Enteric Redmouth (*Yersinia ruckeri),* **ESC** Emphysematous Putrefactive Disease *(Edwardsiella ictaluri),* **BCD** Coldwater Disease (*Flavobacterium psychrophilum),* **CD** Columnaris (*Flavobacterium columnare),* **RS** BKD (*Renibacterium salmoninarum),* **WD** Whirling Disease (*Myxobolus cerebralis*), **CS** Salmonid Ceratomyxosis (*Ceratomyxa shasta).*